BRYCE CANYON
National Park

by Ruth Radlauer

Photographs by
Ed and Ruth Radlauer

Design and map by Rolf Zillmer

AN ELK GROVE BOOK

 CHILDRENS PRESS, CHICAGO

27528

Irene Ingle Public Library
P.O. Box 679
Wrangell, Alaska 99929

Every national park is a BEQUEST OF BEAUTY,
a gift for those who follow.
It is a place of special interest or
beauty that has been set aside by the
United States government especially for you,
your children, and their great-great-grandchildren.
This bequest is yours to have and to care for,
so that others who follow can do the same
during their lives.

Cover: Thor's Hammer

With special thanks to the personnel
at Bryce Canyon National Park

Library of Congress Cataloging in Publication Data

Radlauer, Ruth Shaw.
  Bryce Canyon National Park.
  (Parks for people)
  "An Elk Grove book."
  SUMMARY: Describes the history, sights, and
facilities of Bryce Canyon National Park in Utah.
  1. Bryce Canyon National Park—Juvenile literature.
[1. Bryce Canyon National Park. 2. National parks
and reserves] I. Radlauer, Edward. II. Zillmer,
Rolf. III. Title.
F832.B9R32   917.92'51   79-22722
ISBN 0-516-07484-9

1 2 3 4 5 6 7 8 9 10 11 12 13 14 15 R 86 85 84 83 82 81 80

Contents

What is Bryce Canyon National Park?

Bryce Canyon National Park is a showcase of towers and spires carved out of pink cliffs. It's a story of erosion by snow, ice, and rainstorms.

Some of the tall, narrow formations look like church steeples. Others are castles. You may think you see hundreds of chess pieces carved out of rosy rock. Here's a king, and there's another. The queen even has a garden.

But there's more. Bryce Canyon is a Clark's Nutcracker squawking at you from a Douglas-fir. It may be a white-tail prairie dog standing up to stare at you. And if you watch carefully, you'll see mule deer grazing in a meadow.

This park is a rim walk with a park ranger, or a horse ride on Peekaboo Loop Trail.

Bryce is a bristlecone pine clinging to a dry, windy ridge. It's a blue columbine beside a sandy trail.

Yes, morning, noon, or night, Bryce Canyon is a treat for the eyes. At sunrise the canyon is alive with red, pink, and orange. Mid-day brings the endless deep blue of the sky. And brilliant stars pierce the black sky that covers the canyon at night.

Chess, Anyone?

Clark's Nutcracker

Ride Past The Wall Of Windows

Blue Columbine

Your Trip to Bryce Canyon

All these wonders of Bryce Canyon are in southwestern Utah. From Las Vegas, Nevada, you can go north on Interstate Highway 15, east on Utah 9 through Zion National Park, and north on 89. From Salt Lake City, Utah, take I-15 south to 89. At Bryce Junction, Highway 12 takes you east to the park entrance.

For a daily fee, you can stay in one of two campgrounds. They're open from May to November, but by October, outdoor water pipes freeze. Since no one is allowed to gather firewood, you must bring your own. Space cannot be reserved, so it's best to arrive at the campground very early in the day.

From mid-June through Labor Day, you can reserve a room in the lodge. Write to TWA Services, Inc., P.O. Box 400, Cedar City, Utah 84720.

Because of Bryce's high altitude, you'll want warm clothes and a sun hat. Sweaters and a light jacket will let you peel off layers as it gets warmer. If you hike, you need sturdy shoes or boots and a canteen.

For a map and more information, write the Superintendent, Bryce Canyon National Park, Bryce Canyon, Utah 84717.

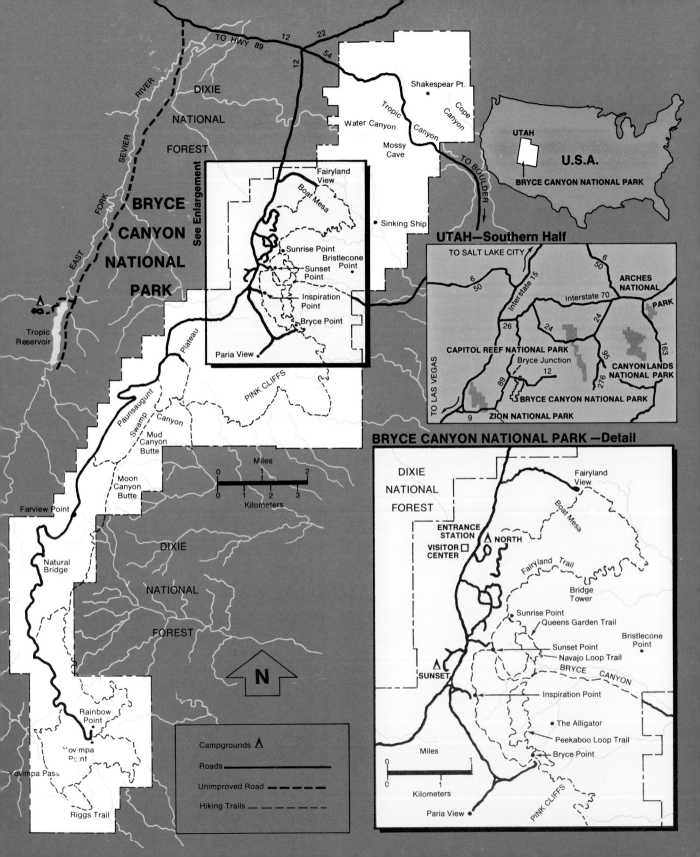

TO HWY 89

12
22
54
12

DIXIE

NATIONAL

FOREST

Shakespear Pt.

Cope
Canyon

Tropic
Canyon

Water Canyon

Mossy
Cave

Sinking Ship

TO BOULDER

UTAH

U.S.A.

BRYCE CANYON NATIONAL PARK

SEVER RIVER

EAST FORK

BRYCE
CANYON
NATIONAL
PARK

See Enlargement

Fairland
View

Boat Mesa

Sunrise Point

Bristlecone
Point

Sunset
Point

Inspiration
Point

Bryce Point

Paria View

Tropic
Reservoir

Plateau

PINK CLIFFS

Paunsaugunt

Swamp Canyon

Mud
Canyon
Butte

Moon
Canyon
Butte

Farview Point

Natural
Bridge

DIXIE

NATIONAL

FOREST

Miles
0   1   2
0   1   2   3
Kilometers

Rainbow
Point

Yovimpa
Point

Yovimpa Pass

Riggs Trail

Campgrounds ⛺

Roads

Unimproved Road

Hiking Trails

UTAH—Southern Half

TO SALT LAKE CITY

6
50

6
50

Interstate 15

Interstate 70

ARCHES
NATIONAL
PARK

26

24

24

95

163

CAPITOL REEF NATIONAL PARK

Bryce Junction

276

CANYONLANDS
NATIONAL
PARK

TO LAS VEGAS

89

12

BRYCE CANYON NATIONAL PARK

9

ZION NATIONAL PARK

BRYCE CANYON NATIONAL PARK —Detail

DIXIE
NATIONAL
FOREST

Fairland
View

Boat Mesa

ENTRANCE
STATION

VISITOR
CENTER

⛺ NORTH

Fairland Trail

Bridge
Tower

Sunrise Point

Queens Garden Trail

Sunset Point

Bristlecone
Point

Navajo Loop Trail

BRYCE   CANYON

⛺
SUNSET

Inspiration Point

The Alligator

Peekaboo Loop Trail

Bryce Point

Miles
0   1
0   1
Kilometers

Paria View

PINK CLIFFS

N

Fairyland

After the long drive, you can hardly wait to see the famous rock formations. Just inside the park, a sign leads you to Fairyland for your first look.

There before you, almost as far as you can see, are rocks, standing at attention. Some have names. Off to your left are tilted layers of rock. That's Sinking Ship, and you'll hear a lot about it during your stay. To your right is Boat Mesa, a good place to hike with a park ranger.

But you don't have to learn the names. You can let your imagination run wild. What will you call the tower with a flat top where a sentry might stand to guard a fairy castle? Maybe you'll see a fort you can name after yourself. Do you see a dog barking at a lion? What will you call the hundreds of fingers pointing to the clouds?

The shapes are very strange. And as you stand and stare, you'll probably wonder, "How did Bryce Canyon take this amazing shape?"

Layers of Time

How did Bryce Canyon become a land of fantastic stone statues? Some questions will be answered when you go to the Visitor Center museum. And you'll hear more when you join a park ranger on a guided walk.

You'll learn that about 60 million years ago, a huge lake covered much of southern Utah. From higher land, streams, rivers, and sudden downpours washed sand, silt, and lime into that lake, scientists now call Lake Flagstaff.

These materials sank to the bottom of the lake as layers of sediment. For awhile one kind of sediment may have come from the north. Then another kind might come from the east. From all directions, different sediments were carried into the lake.

This went on for millions of years. A chemical found in lime filtered through most of the layers and cemented the particles together. The layers became a kind of sedimentary rock called limestone.

But each layer was different. Some were very soft, some hard, and others very hard limestone.

Layers Of Sediments Became Limestone ▶

The Earth Rises

After millions of years, Lake Flagstaff filled with sediments and dried out. The sediments packed down and hardened into what earth scientists, geologists, have named the Wasatch Formation.

Then about 13 million years ago, the earth's crust began to move. Slowly, over millions of years, it quaked while some gigantic force within the earth lifted a huge area. This uplifted chunk of land included southwestern Colorado, northwestern New Mexico, northern Arizona, and southern Utah. All of this region is now known as the Colorado Plateau.

During the uplift, the Colorado Plateau itself broke into blocks that are many kilometers across. Erosion separated these blocks and each one became a tableland, or plateau.

Several of these blocks, or plateaus, contain the Wasatch Formation. On the Paunsaugunt Plateau, the Wasatch is the uppermost layer where the amazing shapes of Bryce Canyon are carved.

Now you may ask, ''What were the tools that some master carver used to shape these countless works of art?''

page 12

Carving Tools

The whole earth is carved, or eroded, by rain, snow, and ice. It is also weathered by plant roots, by chemicals, and by the burrowing of animals. The shape that's left after erosion depends on the makeup of the soil or rock and the tools that do the carving.

At Bryce the winter snow piles on top of the rocks. When the sun comes out, melted snow flows into cracks. At night the water freezes. As water freezes, it expands and pushes the rocks apart. Pieces break off and crash to the earth below. In summer, heavy rain washes the winter's collection of broken rocks into the Paria Valley below Bryce Canyon.

These are the tools that carve the different layers of the Wasatch Formation. Some layers are harder than others and erode slowly. Soft layers wash away more rapidly. When soft rocks are protected from rain by caps of harder limestone, they erode more slowly.

Where the rock is soft, grooves, scallops, and niches are carved out. Harder layers become knobs, bulges, and ledges.

The Sentinel—Carved By Erosion ▶

The Fall of Giants

Special tools have carved a special place. But when will the "master carver" be done with the job? Maybe never.

As long as rain and snow fall on southern Utah, the rocks will erode. Heavy summer rains wash boulders, gravel, and sand along the bases of these rosy monuments. This material scours slanted grooves in the rocks.

At times the water and tumbling rocks grind away at the base of a tower and it falls. If a formation loses its cap rock, it may crumble. Bit by bit the crumbled rock forms rounded hills called badlands because little will grow on them. Much of the rock joins a muddy torrent rushing down the gullies to the Paria Valley.

But as these giants fall, more are being created at the canyon's rim. Erosion gnaws at the edge of the canyon. Bits slide away and form wavy ravines. Eventually, the ravines wash away, laying bare the rock beneath them.

By now you know what comes next: more erosion. Snow, water, and ice begin carving rock ridges and fins which will one day be new works of Bryce Canyon art.

Tower Undermined By Rushing Water

Crumbled Monuments Make Badlands

Ravines Wash Away To Reveal Ridges And Fins

Ebenezer's Glory

Ancient people probably saw the carvings of Bryce Canyon. Much later, Paiute Indians claimed most of southern Utah. Often raided by Utes and Navajos, the Paiutes defended their right to the game and vegetation.

Then came the settlers with horses, cattle, and sheep that pushed game animals off the range lands. Settlers hunted deer, but if Paiutes "hunted" beef cattle, they were punished.

The Paiutes joined the Navajos and Utes to fight against the settlers in the Black Hawk War. But finally, in 1872, agreements brought peace. Southern Utah became farm, ranch, and lumbering country.

In 1874, Ebenezer Bryce settled on a stream that drained a canyon full of towering rocks. "Ebenezer's Glory" was soon known as Bryce's Canyon. But the cows strayed among the rocks, and crops were poor. Soon Mr. Bryce moved away.

Later, Bryce Canyon was rediscovered by people who believed it was a wonder to be preserved. It became a national park in 1928. And now you can be one of many who pitch a tent and stay awhile to enjoy "Ebenezer's Glory."

Indians Hunted With Bows And Arrows

Horn For Gun Powder—Can For Baking Powder

Today's Settler?

Environmental Education

Bryce Canyon took millions of years to form, so you may need several days to get to know it. A good place to start is the Environmental Education building. Young people from 6 to 12 years old can go there every weekday for special park activities.

Every program is different. One day you might go on a geology walk and talk about the Wasatch Formation. Another day you'll take a nature walk and learn the names of flowers and trees.

At the Environmental Education building, you can see a butterfly collection and several birds' nests. You can also get a close look at some study skins. These are skins of animals killed by cars or in other accidents. Often called "road kills," the animals are cleaned and stuffed for study. A gray fox, a skunk, many birds, and squirrels are among the skins you can study.

At another session in this program, you can learn about animal habits. If you learn where they live and what they eat, you'll be more likely to see the real live, year-round residents of Bryce Canyon National Park.

Use Study Skins To Learn About Animals ▶

Animal Watching

Knowing animal habits may help you find some to watch. It helps to know a short-horned lizard has no built-in heating or cooling system. It hides in the shade when it's hot and goes underground when it's cold.

This small, prickly reptile eats grasshoppers, ants, and other insects. These facts tell you to choose a warm day and to find a buggy place to hunt for a horned lizard.

There are many mule deer at Bryce, but insects and heat bother them a lot. Deer browse on herbs, bitterbrush, and manzanita. So where would you go at what time of day to look for deer?

All animals must watch carefully for predators, other animals that kill and eat them. The deer in this national park have few predators. Without predators, the deer population could grow too big, eat up all the browse, and starve. But so far, they only keep the meadows cropped and open to sunshine.

Predators are an important part of nature. They keep a natural balance. Mountain lions, bobcats, and coyotes prey on weak, young, and old animals. Their predation keeps herds of deer or elk healthy and strong.

Young Short-Horned Lizard

Mule Deer

Prairie Dogs

Mice, gophers, prairie dogs, and other rodents could overrun the world without predators to control them. Eagles, owls, and hawks prey on them. But early settlers killed these birds to protect their chickens.

With fewer predators, prairie dog populations grew and grew. Then ranchers and government agents tried to wipe them out. But in 1972, this rodent was put on the list of endangered animals.

The National Park Service and Utah State University are now working to save the white-tail prairie dog. Since 1975, they have tried to transplant colonies of them in Bryce Canyon National Park. By 1978, it looked as though the cat-size rodent would survive.

Prairie dogs live in a system of burrows called dogtowns. They dig their burrows near a good supply of low-growing grass from which they get moisture as well as food. Tall grass would make it too hard to stand up and "talk" to neighboring prairie dogs or to watch for predators.

If you see some mounds in a meadow, watch for them to stand up and chuckle to each other. But take care not to disturb Bryce's newest year-round resident.

Eyes High On The Skull Watch For Flying Predators ▶

Marmots

The yellow-bellied marmot is a bigger rodent than the prairie dog. Both are close relatives in the squirrel family.

There may be several burrows in a marmot colony. Marmots live singly or in pairs in a burrow. They spend their summer wearing paths between lookouts, burrows, and feeding places. On the lookout, a marmot soaks up sunshine while it keeps a wary eye out for badgers and other predators.

A marmot needs a layer of fat to get through the winter. All summer it eats grass, clover, and flowers. In autumn, the marmot seals itself in the burrow to hibernate. During hibernation, breathing slows and the heart rate and body temperature drop.

In the spring, marmots come out of hibernation and begin to eat and mate. One month later, a mother gives birth to about five naked babies with tightly closed eyes. Four weeks later, the babies are covered with fur and have wide-open, beady black eyes.

As spring and summer flowers bloom, the marmot family goes about its eating. By autumn, the young have gone off to the business of digging new burrows for the long winter sleep.

Mother And Baby—Yellow-Bellied Marmot

Eight Beady Black Eyes Peek Out

Have a Safe Time

Any time you watch wildlife, you need to think of safety for the animals as well as yourself.

When you see deer or marmots, you may want to pet them. But any wild animal is dangerous. If a deer is cornered, it will lash out with its sharp hoofs. Mother animals are especially fierce when they have young to protect.

At Bryce, some of the golden-mantled ground squirrels and chipmunks have learned to beg. They love the salt found on people food. But salt takes the moisture out, or dehydrates, their bodies. With very little water here, an animal that eats salt could die of dehydration.

If a squirrel takes your bread crust to its den, the food rots and becomes unfit to eat. The squirrel should be storing seeds and grasses instead of peanuts and potato chips.

In fact, these sweet-looking animals can be a danger to you. Sometimes they have fleas and ticks that carry diseases to humans. And don't let these cute little beggars lure you past the railings along the rim where you could slip and fall. Even *you* can't make a soft landing at the bottom of a 100-meter cliff.

"Please Don't Feed Me" ▶

Rangers

In every national park, you will find some very special people, the park rangers. They can tell you almost everything you want to know about the park.

Rangers take groups of people on walks and give evening programs in the Visitor Center and at North and Sunset amphitheaters.

Many rangers have studied plants, or botany. They've learned about the earth and rock formations in geology classes. One ranger may be an expert on animal behavior. Another can name a bird from only hearing its song.

These people are also trained in safety and first aid. Because of Bryce's high altitude, they carry oxygen in their packs in case someone hikes too hard. A small two-way radio allows him or her to call for help in an emergency.

Boat Mesa, Navajo Loop, Swamp Canyon, Rainbow Point: these are guided hikes you can take with a ranger. As you enter the park, you get a map and a list of activities offered. To give your trip to Bryce more meaning and fun, look for a schedule of these activities posted at the Visitor Center and campgrounds.

Flowers

On a guided walk, you can learn the names of Bryce Canyon flowers. To the Indians, who were the first summer visitors on the Paunsaugunt Plateau, flowers were very important.

The sego lily was sacred in legend. At the same time, Indians dug up sego lily bulbs to eat. They taught the settlers how to use this lily which later became the Utah state flower.

Arrowleaf balsamroot had many uses. Indians ate the roots after washing and boiling them many times to take out the bitter taste. Boiling balsamroot also produced a medicine for headaches and rheumatism. The seeds of the flower were ground into meal to make gruel.

Blue flax blossoms wave gracefully atop long slender stems. But these flowers also produce seeds that Indians used to add extra value and flavor to other foods. They made fishing lines from the fibers in the stems. And they soaked leaves and stems of blue flax to make treatments for swellings, eye infections, and stomach aches.

To the Indians, plants and flowers meant food and medicine as well as beauty.

Sego Lily—Indian Food, Utah State Flower

Arrowleaf Balsamroot—Food And Medicine

Blue Flax—Beauty, Fishing Line, Food, Medicine

Telling Trees

The trees in Bryce Canyon National Park tell us many things. Do you want to know your altitude? If you're looking at pinyons and junipers, you know you're between 1830 and 2430 meters above sea level. At the campground, the ponderosa pines say you're at about 2440 meters. When you see spruce and fir near Rainbow Point, you're above 2750 meters.

Trees tell the history of weather and even erosion. By taking a sample core from a tree, scientists can count the rings and tell how old a tree is. Using the width of the rings, they know how wet the weather was in A.D. 800.

These scientists like to study limber and bristlecone pines because they grow more slowly and live longer than most trees.

At Bryce Canyon, a limber pine clings to the rim at Sunrise Point. It's believed this tree began growing when the rim was several meters beyond it. The tree was probably quite old before the rim eroded out from under its roots. Trees like this one tell us the rim is eroding back from the canyon at a rate of about .3 meters in 50 years.

Pinyon Pine

Bristlecone Pine

Limber Pine Tells The Rate Of Erosion

Day Hiking

A few easy guided walks will build up your lungs and legs for harder hikes. But wherever you hike, you need to remember, what goes down must come up! For a start, go down a short way and walk back up for five minutes. You'll soon find out how much harder uphill hiking is at this altitude.

Even a little hill climbing will slow you as you walk along the rim. The rim trail stretches nine kilometers from Fairyland to Bryce Point. From this trail you can see many views of the north end of Bryce Canyon.

If you're ready for more huff and puff, the Queen's Garden Trail goes into the canyon from Sunrise Point. It's a 45-minute hike to the bottom where you can view a rock that looks like a famous statue of Queen Victoria. Fairyland, Navajo, and Peekaboo Loop Trails are harder.

Be sure to take a sun hat and plenty of water on any hike. The trails are well marked. With a park map in your pocket, you won't get lost, and you'll get to know Bryce Canyon from top to bottom.

Navajo Loop Trail ▶

Backpacking

A night at the base of the canyon is a total wilderness experience. For the privilege of counting stars at Bryce, you need to plan carefully.

Weather during your trip could include heat, rain, wind, and even snow. Hikers take care in choosing each item that goes into their packs. One kilogram carried into the canyon may feel like two on the way to the rim.

Besides food, water, and a sleeping bag, you'll want a backpack stove for cooking. Take a shovel to bury body wastes and plastic bags to carry out trash.

Before you start, you must register at the Visitor Center for a free permit. A park naturalist will tell you where you can camp and if the site has water.

Good hikers stay on the trails. Shortcuts cause erosion, so they don't cut switchbacks. For the safety of others, they never throw rocks.

Every year, thousands of people want to hike into an unspoiled wilderness. Try to leave your campsite so clean that even the ravens won't know that you were there.

You Must Carry Up All You Carry Down ▶

Picture
Bryce Canyon

You can take this park home on film. But you may get more out of your camera if you go on a guided photo walk first.

On the walk, you'll find out that picture taking at Bryce is different. There's more light than you think. The sun's rays are stronger and a lot of light reflects off the rocks.

After you learn to read the light, you find out how to put together, or compose, a good picture. Look for interesting shadows and light. When light reflects off a white rock onto one in shadow, you get a nice effect.

If your picture includes a close rock or tree, you capture some of the size of Bryce Canyon. A close subject gives distance to the rest of the scene. And look for something like a trail to lead the viewer's eye into the picture.

Try to give your picture a point of interest that stands out. Pick a high point, a spot of light, or an unusual shape. Otherwise your picture may be flat and disappointing.

Some say you can't take a bad picture at Bryce. Others say, "Bryce is baffling." So maybe you should take home a few postcards, just in case.

Many Shapes, Many Names

Bryce Canyon is full of strange shapes and stranger names. At the edge of the plateau, where two blocks of earth's crust ground against each other, the layers tilted. Someone decided it looked like an ocean liner going under the water. So now we have the Sinking Ship a long way from any ocean. Then another sea-minded person called a nearby plateau Boat Mesa.

Some New Yorker probably named the rocks on Navajo Loop that look like the towering buildings on Wall Street.

But who named Osiris' Temple after the dwelling of the Egyptian god of the dead? And who saw a Hindu Temple from India right here in Bryce Canyon? Then there's Thor's Hammer. Thor, the Norse god of thunder, needed a huge hammer to pound out bolts of lightning.

The Three Wise Men of Bryce Canyon used to have a camel. But a thunderstorm knocked off the camel's head. (Or was it one of Thor's lightning bolts?)

Most of the formations are still unnamed, so now it's your turn. How long would it take you to name all the rocks in Bryce Canyon National Park?

page 42

Wall Street

Through The Window Of Hindu Temple

You Name It

Go Gently by Moonlight

Maybe you can't stay at Bryce long enough to name all the rocks. But the rocks will wait until you come again to gaze at them.

Before you leave, take time to sit beside the rim. Sit there and be glad this park belongs to you and other people of the world.

Take time to feel and smell the fresh breeze on your face. Listen to the swallows and swifts as they swoop and scoop their dinner of insects out of the air. Remember the bristlecone pine, the lizards, and yes, even the mosquitoes.

Will all these things be here when your grandchildren come to Bryce? Will all those trails be there to take them among the proud rosy monuments? What names will your *great* grandchildren dream up for the towers?

How many future people will see the full moon like a white balloon climbing the spires and pinnacles?

Ponder these questions. Then go gently by moonlight as you say goodbye to Bryce Canyon National Park.

Other National Parks in Utah

In ARCHES NATIONAL PARK, you find red rocks eroded into windows, pinnacles, pedestals, and free-standing arches. Beneath these formations, desert wildlife makes its living among pinyons, junipers, cactus, and yucca.

CANYONLANDS NATIONAL PARK has sandstone arches, needles, and fins eroded by two great rivers. The Green and Colorado Rivers meet in the heart of this park.

A story of earth and early humans is told in the geology and petroglyphs of CAPITOL REEF NATIONAL PARK. This "rainbow captured in rock" was established as a national park in 1971.

On your way to Bryce Canyon, you can go through ZION NATIONAL PARK, where ancient sand dunes have been cemented into Navajo sandstone. As with Bryce, Zion's story includes layered sediments, earth uplift, and erosion.

Double Arch—Arches National Park

Taylor Canyon—Canyonlands National Park

Capitol Reef National Park

Checkerboard Mesa—Zion National Park

The Author and Illustrators

Wyoming-born Ruth Radlauer's love affair with national parks began in Yellowstone. During her younger years, she spent her summers in the Bighorn Mountains, in Yellowstone, or on Casper Mountain.

Ed and Ruth Radlauer, graduates of the University of California at Los Angeles, are authors of many books for young people. Along with their adult daughter and sons, they photograph and write about a wide variety of subjects ranging from monkeys to motorcycles.

The Radlauers live in California, where Ruth and Ed spend much of their time in the mountains near Los Angeles.

* * * *

Ruth and Ed are especially grateful to Carl J. Leibel, who published their first books.